Maintenance Tracker

Maintenance Item	Frequency	Dates Preformed				
AC Filter	Quarterly					
Generator	150 HRS					
Roof Seal Check	Semi - Annual					
Lubricate Hitch	Semi - Annual					
Water Heater Rod	Semi - Annual					

Repairs Tracker

Date	Work Performed	Done By	Cost

Maintenance Tracker

Maintenance Item	Frequency	Dates Preformed				
AC Filter	Quarterly					
Generator	150 HRS					
Roof Seal Check	Semi - Annual					
Lubricate Hitch	Semi - Annual					
Water Heater Rod	Semi - Annual					

Repairs Tracker

Date	Work Performed	Done By	Cost

Maintenance Tracker

Maintenance Item	Frequency	Dates Preformed				
AC Filter	Quarterly					
Generator	150 HRS					
Roof Seal Check	Semi - Annual					
Lubricate Hitch	Semi - Annual					
Water Heater Rod	Semi - Annual					

Repairs Tracker

Date	Work Performed	Done By	Cost

Maintenance Tracker

Maintenance Item	Frequency	Dates Preformed				
AC Filter	Quarterly					
Generator	150 HRS					
Roof Seal Check	Semi - Annual					
Lubricate Hitch	Semi - Annual					
Water Heater Rod	Semi - Annual					

Repairs Tracker

Date	Work Performed	Done By	Cost

Maintenance Tracker

Maintenance Item	Frequency	Dates Preformed				
AC Filter	Quarterly					
Generator	150 HRS					
Roof Seal Check	Semi - Annual					
Lubricate Hitch	Semi - Annual					
Water Heater Rod	Semi - Annual					

Repairs Tracker

Date	Work Performed	Done By	Cost

Maintenance Tracker

Maintenance Item	Frequency	Dates Preformed				
AC Filter	Quarterly					
Generator	150 HRS					
Roof Seal Check	Semi - Annual					
Lubricate Hitch	Semi - Annual					
Water Heater Rod	Semi - Annual					

Repairs Tracker

Date	Work Performed	Done By	Cost

Maintenance Tracker

Maintenance Item	Frequency	Dates Preformed				
AC Filter	Quarterly					
Generator	150 HRS					
Roof Seal Check	Semi - Annual					
Lubricate Hitch	Semi - Annual					
Water Heater Rod	Semi - Annual					

Repairs Tracker

Date	Work Performed	Done By	Cost

Maintenance Tracker

Maintenance Item	Frequency	Dates Preformed				
AC Filter	Quarterly					
Generator	150 HRS					
Roof Seal Check	Semi - Annual					
Lubricate Hitch	Semi - Annual					
Water Heater Rod	Semi - Annual					

Repairs Tracker

Date	Work Performed	Done By	Cost

Maintenance Tracker

Maintenance Item	Frequency	Dates Preformed				
AC Filter	Quarterly					
Generator	150 HRS					
Roof Seal Check	Semi - Annual					
Lubricate Hitch	Semi - Annual					
Water Heater Rod	Semi - Annual					

Repairs Tracker

Date	Work Performed	Done By	Cost

Maintenance Tracker

Maintenance Item	Frequency	Dates Preformed				
AC Filter	Quarterly					
Generator	150 HRS					
Roof Seal Check	Semi - Annual					
Lubricate Hitch	Semi - Annual					
Water Heater Rod	Semi - Annual					

Repairs Tracker

Date	Work Performed	Done By	Cost

Maintenance Tracker

Maintenance Item	Frequency	Dates Preformed				
AC Filter	Quarterly					
Generator	150 HRS					
Roof Seal Check	Semi - Annual					
Lubricate Hitch	Semi - Annual					
Water Heater Rod	Semi - Annual					

Repairs Tracker

Date	Work Performed	Done By	Cost

Maintenance Tracker

Maintenance Item	Frequency	Dates Preformed				
AC Filter	Quarterly					
Generator	150 HRS					
Roof Seal Check	Semi - Annual					
Lubricate Hitch	Semi - Annual					
Water Heater Rod	Semi - Annual					

Repairs Tracker

Date	Work Performed	Done By	Cost

Maintenance Tracker

Maintenance Item	Frequency	Dates Preformed				
AC Filter	Quarterly					
Generator	150 HRS					
Roof Seal Check	Semi - Annual					
Lubricate Hitch	Semi - Annual					
Water Heater Rod	Semi - Annual					

Repairs Tracker

Date	Work Performed	Done By	Cost

Maintenance Tracker

Maintenance Item	Frequency	Dates Preformed				
AC Filter	Quarterly					
Generator	150 HRS					
Roof Seal Check	Semi - Annual					
Lubricate Hitch	Semi - Annual					
Water Heater Rod	Semi - Annual					

Repairs Tracker

Date	Work Performed	Done By	Cost

Maintenance Tracker

Maintenance Item	Frequency	Dates Preformed				
AC Filter	Quarterly					
Generator	150 HRS					
Roof Seal Check	Semi - Annual					
Lubricate Hitch	Semi - Annual					
Water Heater Rod	Semi - Annual					

Repairs Tracker

Date	Work Performed	Done By	Cost

Maintenance Tracker

Maintenance Item	Frequency	Dates Preformed				
AC Filter	Quarterly					
Generator	150 HRS					
Roof Seal Check	Semi - Annual					
Lubricate Hitch	Semi - Annual					
Water Heater Rod	Semi - Annual					

Repairs Tracker

Date	Work Performed	Done By	Cost

Maintenance Tracker

Maintenance Item	Frequency	Dates Preformed				
AC Filter	Quarterly					
Generator	150 HRS					
Roof Seal Check	Semi - Annual					
Lubricate Hitch	Semi - Annual					
Water Heater Rod	Semi - Annual					

Repairs Tracker

Date	Work Performed	Done By	Cost

Maintenance Tracker

Maintenance Item	Frequency	Dates Preformed				
AC Filter	Quarterly					
Generator	150 HRS					
Roof Seal Check	Semi - Annual					
Lubricate Hitch	Semi - Annual					
Water Heater Rod	Semi - Annual					

Repairs Tracker

Date	Work Performed	Done By	Cost

Maintenance Tracker

Maintenance Item	Frequency	Dates Preformed				
AC Filter	Quarterly					
Generator	150 HRS					
Roof Seal Check	Semi - Annual					
Lubricate Hitch	Semi - Annual					
Water Heater Rod	Semi - Annual					

Repairs Tracker

Date	Work Performed	Done By	Cost

Maintenance Tracker

Maintenance Item	Frequency	Dates Preformed				
AC Filter	Quarterly					
Generator	150 HRS					
Roof Seal Check	Semi - Annual					
Lubricate Hitch	Semi - Annual					
Water Heater Rod	Semi - Annual					

Repairs Tracker

Date	Work Performed	Done By	Cost

Maintenance Tracker

Maintenance Item	Frequency	Dates Preformed				
AC Filter	Quarterly					
Generator	150 HRS					
Roof Seal Check	Semi - Annual					
Lubricate Hitch	Semi - Annual					
Water Heater Rod	Semi - Annual					

Repairs Tracker

Date	Work Performed	Done By	Cost

Maintenance Tracker

Maintenance Item	Frequency	Dates Preformed				
AC Filter	Quarterly					
Generator	150 HRS					
Roof Seal Check	Semi - Annual					
Lubricate Hitch	Semi - Annual					
Water Heater Rod	Semi - Annual					

Repairs Tracker

Date	Work Performed	Done By	Cost

Maintenance Tracker

Maintenance Item	Frequency	Dates Preformed				
AC Filter	Quarterly					
Generator	150 HRS					
Roof Seal Check	Semi - Annual					
Lubricate Hitch	Semi - Annual					
Water Heater Rod	Semi - Annual					

Repairs Tracker

Date	Work Performed	Done By	Cost

Maintenance Tracker

Maintenance Item	Frequency	Dates Preformed				
AC Filter	Quarterly					
Generator	150 HRS					
Roof Seal Check	Semi - Annual					
Lubricate Hitch	Semi - Annual					
Water Heater Rod	Semi - Annual					

Repairs Tracker

Date	Work Performed	Done By	Cost

Maintenance Tracker

Maintenance Item	Frequency	Dates Preformed				
AC Filter	Quarterly					
Generator	150 HRS					
Roof Seal Check	Semi - Annual					
Lubricate Hitch	Semi - Annual					
Water Heater Rod	Semi - Annual					

Repairs Tracker

Date	Work Performed	Done By	Cost

Maintenance Tracker

Maintenance Item	Frequency	Dates Preformed				
AC Filter	Quarterly					
Generator	150 HRS					
Roof Seal Check	Semi - Annual					
Lubricate Hitch	Semi - Annual					
Water Heater Rod	Semi - Annual					

Repairs Tracker

Date	Work Performed	Done By	Cost

Maintenance Tracker

Maintenance Item	Frequency	Dates Preformed				
AC Filter	Quarterly					
Generator	150 HRS					
Roof Seal Check	Semi - Annual					
Lubricate Hitch	Semi - Annual					
Water Heater Rod	Semi - Annual					

Repairs Tracker

Date	Work Performed	Done By	Cost

Maintenance Tracker

Maintenance Item	Frequency	Dates Preformed				
AC Filter	Quarterly					
Generator	150 HRS					
Roof Seal Check	Semi - Annual					
Lubricate Hitch	Semi - Annual					
Water Heater Rod	Semi - Annual					

Repairs Tracker

Date	Work Performed	Done By	Cost

Maintenance Tracker

Maintenance Item	Frequency	Dates Preformed				
AC Filter	Quarterly					
Generator	150 HRS					
Roof Seal Check	Semi - Annual					
Lubricate Hitch	Semi - Annual					
Water Heater Rod	Semi - Annual					

Repairs Tracker

Date	Work Performed	Done By	Cost

Maintenance Tracker

Maintenance Item	Frequency	Dates Preformed				
AC Filter	Quarterly					
Generator	150 HRS					
Roof Seal Check	Semi - Annual					
Lubricate Hitch	Semi - Annual					
Water Heater Rod	Semi - Annual					

Repairs Tracker

Date	Work Performed	Done By	Cost

Maintenance Tracker

Maintenance Item	Frequency	Dates Preformed				
AC Filter	Quarterly					
Generator	150 HRS					
Roof Seal Check	Semi - Annual					
Lubricate Hitch	Semi - Annual					
Water Heater Rod	Semi - Annual					

Repairs Tracker

Date	Work Performed	Done By	Cost

Maintenance Tracker

Maintenance Item	Frequency	Dates Preformed				
AC Filter	Quarterly					
Generator	150 HRS					
Roof Seal Check	Semi - Annual					
Lubricate Hitch	Semi - Annual					
Water Heater Rod	Semi - Annual					

Repairs Tracker

Date	Work Performed	Done By	Cost

Maintenance Tracker

Maintenance Item	Frequency	Dates Preformed				
AC Filter	Quarterly					
Generator	150 HRS					
Roof Seal Check	Semi - Annual					
Lubricate Hitch	Semi - Annual					
Water Heater Rod	Semi - Annual					

Repairs Tracker

Date	Work Performed	Done By	Cost

Maintenance Tracker

Maintenance Item	Frequency	Dates Preformed				
AC Filter	Quarterly					
Generator	150 HRS					
Roof Seal Check	Semi - Annual					
Lubricate Hitch	Semi - Annual					
Water Heater Rod	Semi - Annual					

Repairs Tracker

Date	Work Performed	Done By	Cost

Maintenance Tracker

Maintenance Item	Frequency	Dates Preformed				
AC Filter	Quarterly					
Generator	150 HRS					
Roof Seal Check	Semi - Annual					
Lubricate Hitch	Semi - Annual					
Water Heater Rod	Semi - Annual					

Repairs Tracker

Date	Work Performed	Done By	Cost

Maintenance Tracker

Maintenance Item	Frequency	Dates Preformed				
AC Filter	Quarterly					
Generator	150 HRS					
Roof Seal Check	Semi - Annual					
Lubricate Hitch	Semi - Annual					
Water Heater Rod	Semi - Annual					

Repairs Tracker

Date	Work Performed	Done By	Cost

Maintenance Tracker

Maintenance Item	Frequency	Dates Preformed				
AC Filter	Quarterly					
Generator	150 HRS					
Roof Seal Check	Semi - Annual					
Lubricate Hitch	Semi - Annual					
Water Heater Rod	Semi - Annual					

Repairs Tracker

Date	Work Performed	Done By	Cost

Maintenance Tracker

Maintenance Item	Frequency	Dates Preformed				
AC Filter	Quarterly					
Generator	150 HRS					
Roof Seal Check	Semi - Annual					
Lubricate Hitch	Semi - Annual					
Water Heater Rod	Semi - Annual					

Repairs Tracker

Date	Work Performed	Done By	Cost

Maintenance Tracker

Maintenance Item	Frequency	Dates Preformed				
AC Filter	Quarterly					
Generator	150 HRS					
Roof Seal Check	Semi - Annual					
Lubricate Hitch	Semi - Annual					
Water Heater Rod	Semi - Annual					

Repairs Tracker

Date	Work Performed	Done By	Cost

Maintenance Tracker

Maintenance Item	Frequency	Dates Preformed				
AC Filter	Quarterly					
Generator	150 HRS					
Roof Seal Check	Semi - Annual					
Lubricate Hitch	Semi - Annual					
Water Heater Rod	Semi - Annual					

Repairs Tracker

Date	Work Performed	Done By	Cost

Maintenance Tracker

Maintenance Item	Frequency	Dates Preformed				
AC Filter	Quarterly					
Generator	150 HRS					
Roof Seal Check	Semi - Annual					
Lubricate Hitch	Semi - Annual					
Water Heater Rod	Semi - Annual					

Repairs Tracker

Date	Work Performed	Done By	Cost

Maintenance Tracker

Maintenance Item	Frequency	Dates Preformed				
AC Filter	Quarterly					
Generator	150 HRS					
Roof Seal Check	Semi - Annual					
Lubricate Hitch	Semi - Annual					
Water Heater Rod	Semi - Annual					

Repairs Tracker

Date	Work Performed	Done By	Cost

Maintenance Tracker

Maintenance Item	Frequency	Dates Preformed				
AC Filter	Quarterly					
Generator	150 HRS					
Roof Seal Check	Semi - Annual					
Lubricate Hitch	Semi - Annual					
Water Heater Rod	Semi - Annual					

Repairs Tracker

Date	Work Performed	Done By	Cost

Maintenance Tracker

Maintenance Item	Frequency	Dates Preformed				
AC Filter	Quarterly					
Generator	150 HRS					
Roof Seal Check	Semi - Annual					
Lubricate Hitch	Semi - Annual					
Water Heater Rod	Semi - Annual					

Repairs Tracker

Date	Work Performed	Done By	Cost

Maintenance Tracker

Maintenance Item	Frequency	Dates Preformed				
AC Filter	Quarterly					
Generator	150 HRS					
Roof Seal Check	Semi - Annual					
Lubricate Hitch	Semi - Annual					
Water Heater Rod	Semi - Annual					

Repairs Tracker

Date	Work Performed	Done By	Cost

Maintenance Tracker

Maintenance Item	Frequency	Dates Preformed				
AC Filter	Quarterly					
Generator	150 HRS					
Roof Seal Check	Semi - Annual					
Lubricate Hitch	Semi - Annual					
Water Heater Rod	Semi - Annual					

Repairs Tracker

Date	Work Performed	Done By	Cost

Maintenance Tracker

Maintenance Item	Frequency	Dates Preformed				
AC Filter	Quarterly					
Generator	150 HRS					
Roof Seal Check	Semi - Annual					
Lubricate Hitch	Semi - Annual					
Water Heater Rod	Semi - Annual					

Repairs Tracker

Date	Work Performed	Done By	Cost

Maintenance Tracker

Maintenance Item	Frequency	Dates Preformed				
AC Filter	Quarterly					
Generator	150 HRS					
Roof Seal Check	Semi - Annual					
Lubricate Hitch	Semi - Annual					
Water Heater Rod	Semi - Annual					

Repairs Tracker

Date	Work Performed	Done By	Cost

Maintenance Tracker

Maintenance Item	Frequency	Dates Preformed				
AC Filter	Quarterly					
Generator	150 HRS					
Roof Seal Check	Semi - Annual					
Lubricate Hitch	Semi - Annual					
Water Heater Rod	Semi - Annual					

Repairs Tracker

Date	Work Performed	Done By	Cost

Maintenance Tracker

Maintenance Item	Frequency	Dates Preformed				
AC Filter	Quarterly					
Generator	150 HRS					
Roof Seal Check	Semi - Annual					
Lubricate Hitch	Semi - Annual					
Water Heater Rod	Semi - Annual					

Repairs Tracker

Date	Work Performed	Done By	Cost

Maintenance Tracker

Maintenance Item	Frequency	Dates Preformed				
AC Filter	Quarterly					
Generator	150 HRS					
Roof Seal Check	Semi - Annual					
Lubricate Hitch	Semi - Annual					
Water Heater Rod	Semi - Annual					

Repairs Tracker

Date	Work Performed	Done By	Cost

Maintenance Tracker

Maintenance Item	Frequency	Dates Preformed				
AC Filter	Quarterly					
Generator	150 HRS					
Roof Seal Check	Semi - Annual					
Lubricate Hitch	Semi - Annual					
Water Heater Rod	Semi - Annual					

Repairs Tracker

Date	Work Performed	Done By	Cost

Maintenance Tracker

Maintenance Item	Frequency	Dates Preformed				
AC Filter	Quarterly					
Generator	150 HRS					
Roof Seal Check	Semi - Annual					
Lubricate Hitch	Semi - Annual					
Water Heater Rod	Semi - Annual					

Repairs Tracker

Date	Work Performed	Done By	Cost

Maintenance Tracker

Maintenance Item	Frequency	Dates Preformed				
AC Filter	Quarterly					
Generator	150 HRS					
Roof Seal Check	Semi - Annual					
Lubricate Hitch	Semi - Annual					
Water Heater Rod	Semi - Annual					

Repairs Tracker

Date	Work Performed	Done By	Cost

Maintenance Tracker

Maintenance Item	Frequency	Dates Preformed				
AC Filter	Quarterly					
Generator	150 HRS					
Roof Seal Check	Semi - Annual					
Lubricate Hitch	Semi - Annual					
Water Heater Rod	Semi - Annual					

Repairs Tracker

Date	Work Performed	Done By	Cost

Maintenance Tracker

Maintenance Item	Frequency	Dates Preformed				
AC Filter	Quarterly					
Generator	150 HRS					
Roof Seal Check	Semi - Annual					
Lubricate Hitch	Semi - Annual					
Water Heater Rod	Semi - Annual					

Repairs Tracker

Date	Work Performed	Done By	Cost

Maintenance Tracker

Maintenance Item	Frequency	Dates Preformed				
AC Filter	Quarterly					
Generator	150 HRS					
Roof Seal Check	Semi - Annual					
Lubricate Hitch	Semi - Annual					
Water Heater Rod	Semi - Annual					

Repairs Tracker

Date	Work Performed	Done By	Cost

Maintenance Tracker

Maintenance Item	Frequency	Dates Preformed				
AC Filter	Quarterly					
Generator	150 HRS					
Roof Seal Check	Semi - Annual					
Lubricate Hitch	Semi - Annual					
Water Heater Rod	Semi - Annual					

Repairs Tracker

Date	Work Performed	Done By	Cost

Maintenance Tracker

Maintenance Item	Frequency	Dates Preformed				
AC Filter	Quarterly					
Generator	150 HRS					
Roof Seal Check	Semi - Annual					
Lubricate Hitch	Semi - Annual					
Water Heater Rod	Semi - Annual					

Repairs Tracker

Date	Work Performed	Done By	Cost

Maintenance Tracker

Maintenance Item	Frequency	Dates Preformed				
AC Filter	Quarterly					
Generator	150 HRS					
Roof Seal Check	Semi - Annual					
Lubricate Hitch	Semi - Annual					
Water Heater Rod	Semi - Annual					

PAGE 1

Made in the USA
Monee, IL
24 June 2023